T0380976

WHEN PASSION BLOSSOMS

Rosetta Hill-Bennett

ISBN: Softcover   978-1-7960-4376-1
        EBook   978-1-7960-4375-4

Design & Creative Direction: Liandra Bennett

Print information available on the last page

Rev. date: 06/28/2019

To order additional copies of this book, contact:
Xlibris
1-888-795-4274
www.Xlibris.com
Orders@Xlibris.com

Contents

The Passion Vine

All life has purpose. It is a power that is beyond measure. A God given determination to thrive in spite of circumstances and situations. A will to go on; to push through and overcome. The word emotion does not define its many qualities. It is much more. It is the manifested glory of God abounding in everything to fulfill its purpose. A force that has within it meaning, beauty, desire, dreams, aspirations, ambition, ideas, and hope. A strength to grow and blossom according to His plan. All creatures possess this drive to flourish and become useful in its own way.

For instance, in the plant world, there are many unique and beautiful flowers but none so lovely and interesting as the Passion Vine. The Passion flower, also known as Passiflora, has approximately 550 species. It produces regularly and is showy with beautiful and distinctive coronas. It is a common roadside weed that is found throughout Southeastern USA. Although, a wild flower, with striking beauty, it has the potential to produce a fleshy sweet fruit. This perennial climbing vine typically grows in Europe, as well. Its common names are maypop, apricot vine, passion vine, and passiflore.

The flower is not only a beautiful, but it has a calming nature, as well as its calming name (passion). It also has many positive benefits, and natural healing purposes, such as, calming anxieties, inflammation, skin irritations, burns, menopause, ADHD and even more serious conditions, like seizures, high blood pressure and asthma. It is also beneficial in flavoring foods, infusions, teas, liquid extracts, and tinctures. It is believed to be just as effective as synthetic drugs for anxiety disorders (GAD). Studies of the flower has found in it certain compounds that interact with some brain receptors provoking relaxation. Further studies found it to reduce insulin levels and improve sleep disorders.

What a lovely illustration the passion vines give, of a purpose driven life. A life that thrives to bloom, despite its location, and environment, a vine that brings forth lovely blossoms and fruit, in-spite of its inferior description as a weed. A plant that has so many useful qualities, as well as beauty, that it runs with determination to bless the world. Eager to spread its buds in awesome splendor in fields, ditches and roadsides despite its difficulties. Like the passion vine, we all have beauty, purpose and usefulness. There are no exceptions. Everyone has the God given ability to rise and bloom. Nonetheless, how, when, and where we bloom is all up to us. As for age, we can never be too old or too young to have passion. Passion burns eternally, and its flames are hot with aspiration and hope. A potential that surpasses our understanding and reasoning. Inasmuch, as the passion seed that rises in-spite of the pounds of soil that holds it down. We too must rise despite life's weights and obstacles. Armed with faith, to push forth and sprout our buds. Ultimately, beautifying the world with our petals of ideas, dreams, and inspirations. Finally becoming all that we were meant to be, fulfilling our mission like the beautiful passion vine that grows in unusual places.

Passion

Flowers

Sprout

With

Grace

Passion Blossom

She stands regal in the sunlight, without a sound-
A bud that has quietly emerged from the ground-
Her true beauty awaiting, with great expectation-
To open her splendid petals of rich imagination-
Gradually she awakens, as a dream long undone-
Her petals extended as if praising the bright sun-
At last there's understanding as clear as a loom-
A passion has blossomed and is in full bloom-

Passion Vines

How wonderful it is to see-
A passion vine that runs so free-
A vine that swoops and never yields-
Unrestrained through far open fields-
Scattering its beauty wherever it goes-
Embracing the bright sun as it grows-
Up and down it spreads like a fire-
Over hills and dells with pure desire-
Gracing the world with its many buds-
That glisten in the sun like soapy suds-

Spring Vines

In spring the sprawling Maypops are simply divine.

And the ditches are covered with the Apricot Vine.

Dainty white blossoms entwined like fine lace,

Scatter without mercy from place to place.

Delicate buds open wide for Bumblebees,

And joyful birds sing in emerald green trees.

A Quiet Stir

Within our hearts lie a quiet stir.

A vision so dim, a dream yet blur.

Waiting so still to push its way out.

To grow at last, and finally sprout.

To open its self for the world to see,

Its glory, wonder and majesty.

A stir that churns for someone who,

Will someday make a dream come true.

Passion

Blossoms

Thrive

to

Bloom

Perspective

As I gaze in the mirror, I just love what I see –
Because the person I see looks just like me –
Amazing and beautiful in my own special way –
For I have a new perspective of myself today –
Perspective's an attitude or the way you feel inside –
That gives a glowing aura of self- respect and pride –
Your outlook changes and there is a different view –
In that something very odd has happened to you –

So, starting my morning, I took the time to pray –
Did an attitude adjustment before I began my day –
Suddenly I was booming from my head to my toes –
And it wasn't my makeup or my designer clothes –
I'm now looking at the world in a very special way –
It's my perspective and I am incredible today-

There's no need for flattery, if you feel worthwhile –
If you are a confident person with a confident style.
You'll be full of assurance, and it'll show your face –

Because something spectacular has taken place –
Your aspect has changed, you feel a different way –
Lighthearted and wonderful throughout the day –

Seeds of kindness

make

beautiful buds

More than a Word

Loneliness is more than just a word –
It's an indistinct cry that goes unheard –
A weary heart that's missing one beat –
A circle that's broken and incomplete –
A wanting or aching with great desire –
To burn with love's hot and indelible fire –
Its many solemn, and despairing faces –
Are often discovered in unusual places –
The elderly person at the corner store –
The neighbors seldom seen anymore –
The child longing for a mom and dad –
To give them love they've never had –
Or maybe someone who need a friend –
Someone who cares with time to spend –
Someone like you with a great big smile –
Kindhearted, ardent, with a loving style –
That takes a little time to greet and say –
Good morning or Good evening!
How are you, today?

Contagious Expression

A contagious expression really defines a smile –
For it has the ability to make a day worthwhile –
Though a wee emotion, it soothes in such a way –
A sad heart may suddenly enjoy a pleasant day –
Grim faces are overwhelmed by its radiant light –
A brilliant implication that everything is right –
Suddenly life's wonderful and hope fills the air –
As grim faces disappear along with dim despair –
Its highly infectious action, always penetrates –
An unyielding heart where gloom originates –
Though its seldom practiced in today's societies –
Its highly recommended if there are anxieties –
For it is very infectious to those you may meet –
Like ordinary people that we meet on the street –

A Special Feeling

There's something very special about this thing called love –
It's a captivating, rejuvenating, a unique gift from above –
Falling in silly places, it totally consumes a waiting heart –
It fills it unmercifully and overwhelms it from the start –
Its charming and incognitos face always looks brand new –
Rendering a sense of freshness and a much sweeter view –
Old bitterness is forgotten and totally erased from mind –
As it recharges the spirit, and tickles the soul like wine –
Many have found happiness in it; but some misery there –
For if its misguided or one-sided, it dies for lack of care –
Yet yearning souls as if under a spell still fall deep inside –
While others wait patiently for it to flow in like a tide –

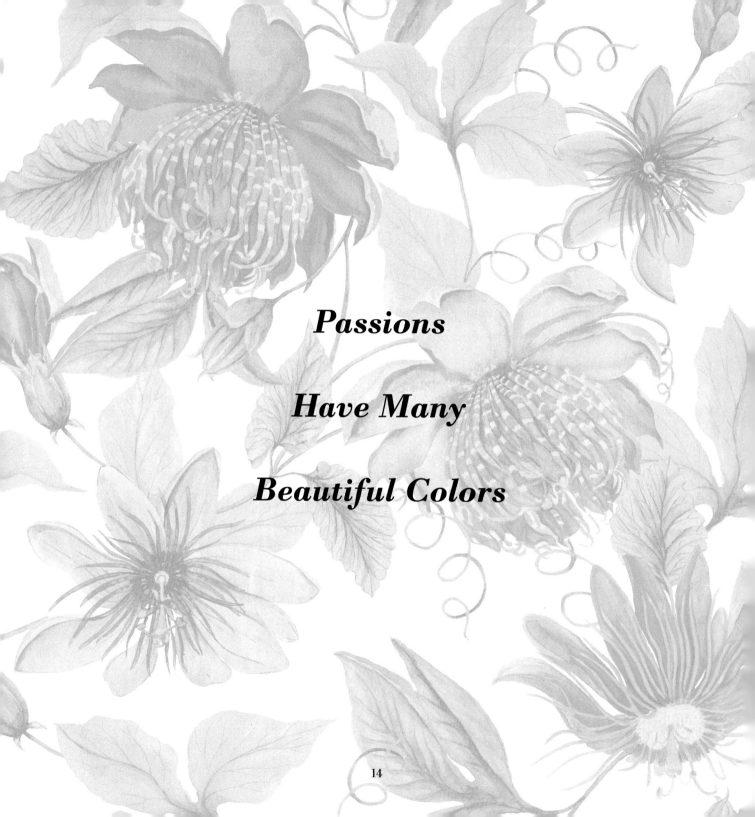

Passions

Have Many

Beautiful Colors

Suppose

Suppose, we were all alike?
How dull the world would be?
If we were all identical,
And there was no variety.
Who would we find to fault;
And who would we blame?
If we were all the one race;
And everyone exactly the same.
Would we finally have tolerance;
Rather than scorn and contempt?
Would prejudices of every kind;
In the whole world be exempt?
Suppose all hate was excluded,
And only love flowed like air;
With kindness and tenderness
In abundance everywhere!!!

The Maple Tree

An amazing place; ideal for me.
Is underneath my maple tree –
For each day when I go there –
I sat to have a morning prayer –
And as I whisper grateful words –
I hear a flock of beautiful birds –
Singing praises in their own way –
Adding such splendor to the day –
A joy unspeakable fills my space –
With peace and such amazing grace –
Amazing Grace how sweet the sound –
That saved a wretch like me –
I once was lost but now I've found –
My place beneath my tree –

The Passion Vine

Flourish

in

Unusual Places

Ole Uncle Bill

It was Saturday afternoon, just before dark,
When I was taking a stroll pass a local park.
When I saw an ole man sitting under a tree.
A funny old man, and as black as can be.
He was known by many as Ole Uncle Bill
Cause to hear him play was such a thrill
His hair was white, and whiskers too.
And his cataract eyes, were almost blue
As he sang and strummed a worn guitar.
It was plain to see; he was no one's star.
Yet the crowd swayed, as under a spell;
He sang real hard, like he'd been in hell
Slow soul tunes, straight from his heart.
As he played a guitar that was falling apart.
Singing and strumming, he patted his feet.
As we clapped hands, along with the beat.
He didn't miss a note, and I felt his pain,
As he played his melodies, again and again.
"Play that blues, Uncle Bill!", I heard somebody say.
Standing in the crowd, listening to the ole man play.
He sang, and played awhile, and when he was done,
The evening darkened quietly, swallowing the sun.
And though time had passed, and it was getting dark
I was feeling quite happy after my day in the park –
Listening and chilling had given me quite the thrill.
What an afternoon it was with good ole Uncle Bill –

Passion Flowers

are

Determined

to

Bloom

The Will

Down throughout the ages the people trod –
 Their path turbulent; their trust in God –
 To survive the hot flames of a bias fire –
 They withstood it with a strong desire –
 A will to live though barred of choices –
 Their cries unheard within still voices –
Struggling on ahead; they blazed a way –
 Our mothers and fathers of yesterday –
 Who showed us how to stand and face –
 To be true to ourselves and run the race –
 Determined to survive, despite despair –
 To live with hope and relentless prayer –

Life

In this life everyone's going through something;
Although some must travel down a different road.
We are all allotted to carry our own individual load.
For it's not easy living; and the rain to all must fall.
Life's made per person, and one size does not fit all.
So, when another's yard look, so bright and green –
Remember that things are not always as they seem.
And count the blessings because you are not alone;
For everyone in this life has their own bed of thorns.
And everyone has the strength no matter how small,
Fortified with faith and courage to withstand it all –

Rain

Makes

Passion

Grow stronger

Hope Glows

Amid the devastation troubles and pain
The losses, and tragedies unrestrained –
Though diseases and poverty rampage on –
Destroying dreams that men have spawned
And schools are riddled, as the bullets fly –
The bombs explode and the innocent die –
And storm winds whirl stronger and faster
Reaping harsh distress and deadly disaster
But despite the vicious and unmerciful blows
Hope like a candle in the darkness yet glows.

Days of Grace

I've had hard days.
I've had easy days;
Some up and down and side-ways
But I've had days
I've had days.
I've had happy days –
And sad days
Good and so-called bad ways
But, I've had days.
I've had abundant days
And lacking days;
Pretty and ugly ways,
But I've had days
I've had days
I've had laughing days,
And crying days;
Sometimes in a funky phase
But, I've had days
I've had days.
I've had days to analyze –
Even theorize and then realize,
That I have lived, to look back and recall;
And I'm grateful for them after-all.
For I've had days in many amazing ways.

A Thing or Two

Listen and I will tell you a thing or two –
Once upon a time I was young like you –
And I could not understand anything
But I found out, what living can bring
By tripping, falling and hanging on,
Working my fingers down to the bone.
And I've had my valleys; mountains, too
But with my courage, I made it through –
There were days of lost and some of gain.
Lord knows I've had, my portion of pain.
But then there were some good days, too –
Nevertheless, there were not that many –
Sometimes need stopped by my house,
A little more frequently, than ole plenty.
But I kept running, though I couldn't see
The thoughts and plans God had for me –
So as a deer caught and blinded by light;
I chose my path, and prayed I was right.
Sometimes I was wrong; I really must say;
I've gained some wisdom along the way.
And because of wisdom, I now understand
That we can only do the best that we can.
For life is a product of choices we make.
Good, or bad are chances that we take.
I know the road, because I've been there
My journey hard, but I made it by prayer
And living has taught me a thing or two;
And in time, I know it will teach you, too.

Time

Brings

Forth

Wonderful

Blossoms

Perpetual

Time lives in yesterday, today and tomorrows.
It's irreversible and never borrows.
Time comes, and time goes –
And how it will leave us –
No one knows.
Time changes; and it will never wait.
It has never been known to procrastinate.
For it is an on- going, perpetual event.
That welcomes opportunities –
With each moment well spent.
And time in its own way,
Miraculously heals;
The pain and sorrows –
That life often yields.
And time, whether in years,
days, hours or minutes,
Can hold the most wonderful –
Moments within it!

Time and Reason

There's a time and reason for everything.
A time for learning;
And a time for teaching.
A time for retracting;
And a time for reaching.
A time for planting.
And a time for growing.
A time of innocence;
And a time of knowing.
A time for suppressing;
And a time for expressing.
A time for standing;
And a time for sitting.
A time to move on;
And a time to stay.
A time of doubt;
And a time to pray.

Peace is where

the

Passion Grows

Optimism

Life's not always
A bed of red roses,
Lillis, daffodils and poses –
For often it's filled with uncertainties and pain –
That test our patience
Again, and again –
Yet despite the contentious
Struggles and sorrow.
There's always the promise
Of a brighter tomorrow –

Passions

Overcome

Mountains

The Legacy

My people were singing people –
Because singing soothes the pain –
Lifting their hearts with melodies –
Time and time again.

My people were dancing people –
Romping and frolicking to be free –
Springing from step to step –
In a spirit of liberty.

My people were praising people –
Rejoicing for the little they had –
Shouting and singing tunefully
Until their souls were glad –

My people were praying people –
Their days were filled with toil –
So, they bent their knees –
Took time to pray –
And burned the mid night oil –

My people were strong people
Emerging through ages with stride –
Leaving behind them a legacy –
Of dignity and pride –

Passion Weeds

Become

Lovely

Blossoms

Printed in the United States
By Bookmasters